The Enlightened Passenger

"You have an illuminated inner self that you can talk to once you read this phenomenal book."

–Mark Victor Hansen, co-founder, *Chicken Soup for the Soul*

"Life gets easier when you're awake for every moment of the journey. *The Enlightened Passenger* will help you in truly embracing the journey."

–James Redfield, *New York Times* Best-selling author, *The Celestine Prophecy*

"If you want to live with your cup constantly in overflow, Corey's new book, *The Enlightened Passenger*, is a must-read."

–Lisa Nichols, *New York Times* Best-selling author, CEO, and founder of Motivating the Masses Inc.

"It's not the 'hows' you need to be concerned with, but the wows. *The Enlightened Passenger* delivers big time on the wows!"

–Mike Dooley, *New York Times* Best-selling author, *Infinite Possibilities*

"This new Parable, by Corey Poirier, teaches the lessons that can take a person from struggling to success."

–Serena Dyer, author, *Don't Die with Your Music Still in You*

"If you want to know how to get what you want, and also how to want what you have, *The Enlightened Passenger* is a must-read."

–John Gray, author, *Men Are from Mars, Women Are from Venus*

"A great book that helps you manifest that which you desire. Put it on your shelf and re-read as necessary."

–Dr. Joe Vitale, author, *Zero Limits* and *The Miracle*

"What you feed your body is of the utmost importance. Feeding your mind the right things is just as important. Corey's book could be the mind food that changes your life forever."

–JJ Virgin, *New York Times* Best-selling author, *The Virgin Diet* and *JJ Virgin's Sugar Impact Diet*

"Corey Poirier's *The Enlightened Passenger* is a captivating journey that transcends the conventional boundaries of success and fulfillment. Through the compelling tale of Robert Stapleton and his unexpected encounter with Trebor, Poirier masterfully weaves a narrative that challenges our perceptions of achievement and purpose. The juxtaposition of Robert's outward success and Treb's life of meaning creates a powerful narrative that resonates with readers on a profound level. Treb's 10 life lessons, delivered with wisdom and simplicity, serve as a transformative guide, leaving an indelible impact on both characters and readers alike. Poirier's writing is reminiscent of the soul-stirring wisdom found in *The Alchemist*, *Celestine Prophecy*, and Og Mandino's timeless classics. *The Enlightened Passenger* is not just a book; it's a transformative experience that invites readers to question, reflect, and embark on their own journey towards a life of true fulfillment. A must-read for those seeking profound insights and a roadmap to a more meaningful existence."

–Debbi Dachinger, award-winning *Dare to Dream* podcast host and journalist, international bestselling author

"I highly recommend Corey's book if you are ready to bring into focus the true gift of life and what it's all about. *The Enlightened Passenger* redefines success in the most beautiful way!"

–Randy Spelling, ReAwaken coach

"You owe it to yourself to learn from the best, and Corey Poirier always brings the HEAT. That's why it's no surprise that so many people will buy, learn, and expand as a result of his new book, *The Enlightened Passenger*."

–John Lee Dumas, host, *Entrepreneurs on Fire*

"I love great books. *The Enlightened Passenger* is what I'd call a great book. You need to make sure you read it this year if you want a great year, because Corey always delivers."

–Anthony Trucks, former NFL linebacker and three-time American Ninja Warrior

"Corey is an amazing interviewer who has collected so much of his discoveries around what it takes to create more happiness, abundance, and a success-filled life."

–Ken Honda, author, *Happy Money*

"Sometimes you start reading a book, and realize you are wasting your time. This is not that book. *The Enlightened Passenger* can change the way you look at happiness and fulfillment."

–Ami James, star, *Miami Ink*

"There are few books that transform you as you read them—*The Enlightened Passenger* is one of them. Each page enlightens the reader with a captivating story and an action to integrate a new conscious practice. Be sure to read to the end for a sweet ending with a surprise twist."

> **–Melanie Bensen,** host of *Amplify Success,* profit and visibility amplifier for expert-preneurs

"It's rare that you find a book that really changes people's lives. Corey has made sure *The Enlightened Passenger* does just that. This is an absolute must-read."

> **–Jon Talarico,** high-performance coach, connector, speaker, and bestselling author

"Your intuition led you to *The Enlightened Passenger* for a reason. Trust it, seize the book, and immerse yourself."

> **–Mas Sajady,** host, *Xponential Intelligence*

"I have had the opportunity to work with many of the world's top influencers, and I have learned that the vast majority read the right books. This is such a book."

> **–Brian Proctor,** author, *My Father Knew the Secret*

The Enlightened
PASSENGER

The Flight That Changes Everything

COREY POIRIER

NEW YORK

LONDON • NASHVILLE • MELBOURNE • VANCOUVER

The Enlightened Passenger

The Flight That Changes Everything

Published in New York, New York, by Morgan James Publishing. Morgan James is a trademark of Morgan James, LLC. www.MorganJamesPublishing.com

Proudly distributed by Publishers Group West®

Morgan James BOGO™

A **FREE** ebook edition is available for you or a friend with the purchase of this print book.

CLEARLY SIGN YOUR NAME ABOVE

Instructions to claim your free ebook edition:
1. Visit MorganJamesBOGO.com
2. Sign your name CLEARLY in the space above
3. Complete the form and submit a photo of this entire page
4. You or your friend can download the ebook to your preferred device

ISBN 9781636984407 paperback
ISBN 9781636984414 ebook
Library of Congress Control Number: 2024933243

Cover Concept by:
Corey Poirier

Morgan James is a proud partner of Habitat for Humanity Peninsula and Greater Williamsburg. Partners in building since 2006.

Get involved today! Visit: www.morgan-james-publishing.com/giving-back

Want to give this book to someone you care about?
Fill in the gift form below, and the recipient
will always remember where they got the book.

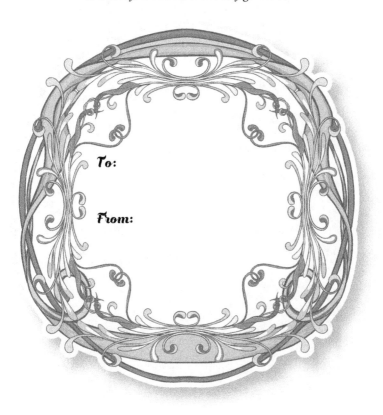

To:

From:

READ THIS FIRST

Grab your free interviews! As a thank you for downloading or purchasing this book, I would like to give you access to two influencer interviews.

To download these interviews—one with the legendary Les Brown, and another with the author of *The Celestine Prophecy*, James Redfield—visit www.coreyonpurpose.com.

And don't forget to visit www.coreypoiriermedia.com for more information about Corey and his work.

DEDICATION

*This book is dedicated to my seatmate, Shelley, who has supported me
in all of my projects and made this book possible in so many ways.
I'd also like to dedicate it to my two sons, Sebastian and Alijah,
who inspire me every day. I love you all so much.
I'd further like to dedicate it to my late grandfather Eddy Doucette;
my late father-in-law, Eric Rogerson; my late grandmother Amy Poirier;
and my grandmother Audrey Doucette.
Last, but not least, thank you to my mother, Nancy, who has taught me
what unconditional love truly means.*

TABLE OF CONTENTS

FOREWORD

I still remember about fifty years ago (I was a shy twelve years old), standing across the concourse of a local mall looking at the man sitting at a table in front of the bookstore. To my surprise, there was nobody in his line. I watched him for nearly twenty minutes, trying to get my courage up to walk across the space and meet him. I didn't have any money for a book, but I wanted to see him up close, hear the actual voice I had only heard in my mind as I read his books, maybe even shake his hand. To touch the hand of a legend.

To my everlasting regret, I let cowardice win and I walked away without meeting him, losing the opportunity to greet a personal hero of mine. The author was Og Mandino, and his book that had impacted me so greatly was called *The Greatest Salesman in the World*, a powerful book that had sold a staggering 50 million copies worldwide. It was the first self-help book I had ever read and, even at that young age, it changed my life. To this day, I still occasionally recite Mandino's ten "scrolls"—mantras that would guide me not only in business but in life. I am forever grateful that I was introduced to a writer like Mr. Mandino. I can say the same about Corey Poirier.

When I first met Corey Poirier, I was impressed with his joyful and friendly demeanor, which I chalked up to him being Canadian (lol). As I got to know him better, I became impressed by his ability to engage and befriend others. He was a natural connector. As I read his biography, that was confirmed. He had the ability to not only bring people together but to bring out the best in them.

We met at a writer's retreat I was hosting. During one of the sessions, he shared with the group the idea of a story he was working on. I was impressed. No. More than that, I was envious. I told him, "If you decide not to write that story, let me know. I will." To my and the world's benefit, Corey wrote that story. *The Enlightened Passenger*.

When I read this short but profound book, I felt as if Og himself had touched Corey and bequeathed upon him the gift of inspiration. The beauty of books like *The Enlightened Passenger* is that they not only make you want to be better; they show you how. And, like *The Greatest Salesman's* ten scrolls, Corey's ten lessons are something that will remain with me.

This book is a gift of heart from a man with a heart. If you're anything like me, I think you'll enjoy not only the lessons learned, but the story itself. Stories change worlds. I think this one could too. Enjoy!

–Richard Paul Evans, #1 *New York Times* and USA Today
Best-selling author

INTRODUCTION

This book that you are reading now simply came through me. That is, it was written by me, but it felt like it was a gift that was given to me, and therefore came through me.

I know I played a part in the writing of it because of the time it took to bring it to life and the writing style, which is similar to the books I favor. They include *The Alchemist* by Paulo Coelho, *The Greatest Salesman in the World* by Og Mandino, *The Celestine Prophecy* by James Redfield, and *The Richest Man in Babylon* by George Samuel Clason. These books changed my life, and certainly inspired this book you are now reading.

I did have the idea for this story long before I sat down to write the book. When you're done of the book, you'll likely be able to figure out how it was inspired.

Each time I found (made?) the time to write, the writing flowed effortlessly and the characters took on their own life. The fact that I had to make the time to write this book, which ended up taking a year, made the book even more special to me. It makes me feel like the book was waiting until the right time to introduce itself to the world.

As you read this book, I hope you see the simplicity yet power in the lessons shared. I would love to take credit for them, but as you'll see, they consist of wisdom I have learned while interviewing many of the world's top influencers and thought leaders.

I don't know that this book will change your life, but I have to believe it has the power to—or I wouldn't feel the need to release it at a time when so many other books are being released.

In reviewing what was shared in these lessons, I thought about whether each one was something I would want my two young sons to know in the future, and unless I answered *yes*, I felt the lesson should be adjusted or removed.

I care about delivering something that can positively impact your life. It is my hope (and goal) that *The Enlightened Passenger* becomes such a thing.

Until then, here's to your greater success (whatever that means to you), my friend.

Corey Poirier
February 2024

Chapter 1:
THE FLIGHT

R obert Stapleton was seated in 9C of the Boeing 747. He was in business class, as usual. Before boarding, he had also made sure—both online and with the desk—that the seat beside him would stay empty. With his laptop open on the table in front of him, he reviewed a spreadsheet full of numbers while listening to music on his earphones.

"Welcome back, Mr. Stapleton," said a voice in the aisle. Robert was so focused on his laptop and music, he didn't realize the flight attendant wanted his attention. She tried again, this time louder. "Welcome back, Mr. Stapleton. Can I get you anything before we take off?"

He still didn't hear her. She simply shook her head and moved down the aisle to the next passenger and asked, "Can I get you something before we take off?" The flight attendant knew Robert tended to stay absorbed in his work. This wasn't the first time she had seen him on a flight—perhaps not surprising, since he often made more than 200 flights a year.

Robert is twenty-five, slim, and dressed in a custom-fitted Armani suit. His Rolex cost more than the average American car. As the regional manager of Lexicomp, he had the role of visiting the company's offices throughout the globe to make sure they had the support of the head office in expanding sales of Lexicomp's photocopiers, printers, and software. Robert also worked to convince the largest customers to buy the newest products. A proud workaholic, he considered it a failure if his personal income was less than $750,000 a year. It often hovered around $1 million.

"Last chance before we take off, Mr. Stapleton ... Robert?" The flight attendant again tried to get his attention. She was just about to walk away when he happened to look over.

"Yes?" he replied, removing his right earphone and holding it in his hand.

"I was just asking if I could get you anything before we take off?"

"Scotch. On the rocks. Neat, as usual," he said.

"More than happy to," she replied, as she made her way to the cart.

Robert put his right earphone back in his ear. As he refocused on his laptop, the flight attendant returned and reached over the empty seat beside him to hand him his drink and a small napkin. Barely looking in her direction, Robert reached out to grab the glass.

"Thanks," was all he offered.

Robert took a couple of sips before placing the glass on his table. Then he shut down the spreadsheet, closed his laptop, and tucked it under his seat. He took his headphones, squished them into a ball in his hands, and shoved them in the seat compartment in front of him. He took a third and final drink from his glass and called the flight attendant over.

"Here, can you take this?" he demanded.

"Sure thing, Mr. Stapleton."

With that, Robert leaned back in his seat and closed his eyes. The flight from New York to London would take about seven hours. He hoped he could have a bit of a nap.

Chapter 2:
THE CONVERSATION

Robert slowly opened his eyes, not knowing how much time had passed. He had clearly slept through takeoff, because when he looked out the window, he could see the Grand Canyon below. There was also now a man sitting in the seat beside him. The man was bald and wearing white clothes that were somehow professional yet relaxed. The man also had a slight but noticeable scar on his right cheek. He looked a little like a slightly more muscular Wayne Dyer, the spiritual influencer who had impacted millions of lives through his books and PBS specials. Robert thought the man was likely in his fifties.

Unlike Robert, the man wasn't wearing a watch. In fact, there seemed to be few similarities between them—except one. Robert noticed the man also had a forearm tattoo of the Om symbol. However, Robert suspected this man had the tattoo for better reasons than he did. Robert had gotten his because he was hanging out with a girl. They had gone to a tattoo shop together, and he had listened when she said it was the coolest tattoo in the artist's catalog, and he should get it.

Robert was adept at looking for similarities between himself and other people in business, a skill that allowed him to build quick and profitable relationships. In this case, however, he was upset to have someone sitting next to him—especially after he had confirmed the seat would be empty. He liked his private time to be private. Had this man snuck into first class?

Before Robert could ask what the man was doing in the seat, the man started talking. "I was wondering when you might wake up. I hope you don't mind me sitting here. I prefer to sit in economy because I love meeting new people. I know people in first class are typically looking to get some rest or get some work done. I guess they oversold the flight. This seat was the only one available, so they bumped me up here!" Then the man leaned over and pointed out the window. "The Grand Canyon. Fascinating, isn't it?"

Robert was still a bit groggy from sleeping. *Boy, this guy likes to talk. Just what I need,* he thought. He planned to tell the man, *I do have a big trip ahead of me, so I think I will go back to sleep.* But before Robert could utter a word, the man reached out his hand to shake Robert's.

"My name is Trebor. I noticed your Rolex. I used to have one just like it."

Robert shook the man's hand, wondering if the man really had owned a similar watch or was just saying so to break the ice or find out how much it was worth. "I'm Robert," he said.

"If you don't mind me asking, what takes you to London? Business?"

Robert started to explain he wanted to sleep. "Look, Trevor …"

"Actually, it's Trebor with a B," the man interjected. "People call me Treb for short."

That's weird, Robert thought, planning again to tell the man he wanted to sleep. Then he recalled another time he'd been forced to sit next to someone on a flight. When they finally began chatting, it turned out the seatmate was a potential customer. Robert even closed a deal on the flight. With that in mind, he opened up his energy and started chatting. "Well, Treb, I'm off to London for work."

"Awesome!" Treb replied. "I used to travel to London for work too. What do you do?"

"I work for a company, Lexicomp. We sell office equipment and products. I'm the regional manager. I travel to different offices to work with the teams there."

"Wow! I used to do something similar."

Robert wondered if Treb was speaking the truth, but he humored him.

"Really?" he asked. "Why did you leave?"

"I struck out on my own. I'd been in the business for a while, and I was CEO. But after we expanded into Europe and the UK, I felt it was time to move on. I went into consulting—in a different field. Now, I work with people one on one."

Robert had his doubts about Treb's story, but he decided there was no harm in playing along. "Did you make a lot of money while you were in the field?" he asked.

"I did quite well," Treb said. "But what I discovered near the end of my career made me *rich*."

Robert was suddenly thankful that he had not gone to sleep.

Chapter 3:
THE FIRST LESSON

The word *rich* had grabbed Robert's attention. Even though he could make up to a million a year, he often spent as much as he earned. He also wanted to become rich enough to strike out on his own, just like this man had. Maybe they did have some similarities after all. Still, he was skeptical about the man's story.

"If I may be blunt, you don't come across as rich," Robert said. "I don't mean to offend you. I'm just curious. I mean, you said you *like* to sit in economy. I don't know one rich person who would choose to sit in economy unless they're cheap," he said, with a chuckle.

Treb smiled. "When I said that I became rich, I didn't mean financially; I meant rich in life."

Great, Robert thought. *I am seated next to a monk.*

"Now," the man continued, "if you measure *rich* by material wealth, I became rich in that way as well. But becoming rich as a person was the real wealth. Mind you, the material part is important! It allowed me to start giving back more."

Whatever floats your boat, Robert thought. But he was still curious—he didn't want to pass up a chance to learn the secrets of wealth. *If the man isn't being honest, that will come out in the conversation, and I can just explain that I'm tired and need another nap,* he thought. Besides, there were many eccentric people who were wealthy beyond belief. Couldn't this man be one of them?

"I'd love to learn more about how you became wealthy," Robert said. Then he looked at his watch and realized they'd been in the air for just about an hour. "I guess we have plenty of time."

Treb leaned in. "I'd be happy to share my story. I wish someone would've shared this stuff with me twenty or thirty years ago. You'll have to bear with a bit of rambling along the way, but I promise I'll get to the money part."

"Great!" Robert replied.

Just as Treb was about to speak, the flight attendant arrived. "Mr. Stapleton, you're up. Can I get you anything?"

"Sure. I'll take a soda pop."

"I'll get right on it," she said. And with that, she disappeared.

"None for me thanks," Treb added with a laugh, after she had left. Then he turned his attention back to Robert. "As far as life lessons, I can start with why I don't drink pop."

Great, here we go. This story is going to be a long one, Robert thought. He turned toward the window and rolled his eyes.

The flight attendant arrived back and handed Robert a can of pop—she knew he preferred to drink out of a can instead of a glass. Then, she continued on to the next row.

"Look, I'm no doctor, and I'm not going to preach about what you eat or drink," Treb said. "I just wanted to share why I stopped drinking the stuff."

"Fine," Robert replied, "but just so you know, I don't drink a lot of pop anyway."

"Have you ever heard of Jack Canfield?" Treb asked.

Robert thought for a minute. "The *Chicken Soup* dude?"

"Exactly. Well, I attended one of his seminars years ago. He talked about how toxic pop is and he used this exercise with a couple of people from the audience. I was one of them. He got me to stand up at the front of the room and hold a can of pop. Then, he asked me to raise my hand, the one holding the pop. He got someone else from the audience to get up on a step stool and push down on my arm, and he told me not to let her push my arm down. I was much larger than her and was pretty sure I would be a lot stronger, but no matter how hard I tried, she pushed my arm down over and over again."

"Maybe it was just the angle she was pushing from," Robert said. "Or the fact she was above you on a stool?"

"You know, that's what I thought. But then Jack got me to hold a glass of water instead of the pop. He asked the woman to push my arm down again. This time, she couldn't, even a bit. I was shocked. Both times, I was resisting but with much different outcomes."

"So what's the point?" Robert asked.

"The point is that the can of pop is negative energy, and when you're working with negative energy, you're weaker. The water is positive energy, and when you're working with positive energy, you're stronger. I drank pop then and didn't see it as negative energy. But I still couldn't hold my arm up."

"So what you're saying is I shouldn't want that negative energy in my body? Is that the idea?"

"You could say I'm simply saying, water good, pop bad. But if you want a better visual, try cleaning a dirty toilet with a can of soda pop. It works every time. So what's it doing to your body? You're a slim kid. You're probably in decent shape. Things change as you age. I'm simply saying if you want to be rich and wealthy—in mind, body, spirit, and money—you need to think about what you're feeding your body." Treb leaned back in. "I mean, what's the point of having a lot of money if you don't have your health? Am I right?"

Robert thought about what Treb had said.

"In fact, that's how Steve Jobs got a beverage company employee to leave and work for Apple," Treb continued.

"What do you mean?" Robert asked.

"Well, Steve was trying to convince the executive to leave. He had interviewed the guy, and the guy was thinking it over. Steve supposedly hit him with one sentence that sealed the deal."

"What was the sentence?"

"He asked the man if he wanted to continue to sell sugared water to kids, or if he wanted to come over to work with Apple and change the world."

"Wow."

"You might not believe the story about me at the Canfield event. But you have a can of pop right here. We can test it."

"Pop or no pop, I don't think you could push my arm down," Robert said with a smirk.

"Let's give it a try. It's not the same as standing up, but let's give it a go anyway."

Robert picked up the can with his left hand and held his arm out.

"Are you ready?" Treb asked.

Robert nodded.

Treb pushed down on Robert's arm. Robert resisted, but his arm flew down so quickly that pop splashed all over the seatback in front of them.

Robert was shocked. He and Treb started to laugh.

After wiping up the spilled pop with Robert's napkin, Treb pulled a refillable water bottle from the seat pocket in front of him.

"This is my water." He handed the bottle to Robert and asked him to raise his arm and hold the bottle the same way he'd held the soda pop.

"Ready?" Treb asked.

Robert nodded again, and Treb again pushed down on his arm. Robert resisted, and his arm barely budged. Robert could hardly believe it. He looked at the half-empty pop can on the tray table and said, "Well, I guess this ends the story of you and I." Then he said, "I'm not sure if I believe in that negative/positive energy stuff, Treb, but I guess I agree pop isn't good for me."

"I actually have ten lessons I share when I'm speaking to people and companies about wealth. You said you're interested in wealth. Are you up for hearing the lessons?"

"What else am I going to do?" Robert said with a laugh. The truth was that if Treb knew anything about becoming rich, Robert wanted to know it too. "I will ask to stop listening if I stop being interested."

"Deal," Treb said, not sure if Robert was being serious or not. "You just had your first lesson. It's not one of the ten, but I'd love you share it with someone."

"What did I just learn?" Robert asked.

"The soda pop experiment. Try it with someone else when you have a chance."

Action: **The Experiment**

1. Get someone to hold out a soda pop. Try to push their arm down while they resist. Then, get the person to hold something like alkaline water and try to push their arm down while they resist. Note the differences in what happens.

Chapter 4:
SYNCHRONICITY

"So, what's Lesson 1?" Robert asked. "Before you share it, you should know I attend a lot of events, so I've probably heard a lot of what you're going to tell me."

"Ever heard of *shoshin*?" Treb asked.

"I don't think so," Robert confessed.

"Years ago, my wife and I took a trip to Japan. When we were there, I was introduced to *shoshin*. Like you, I thought I'd heard of everything. Anyway, my wife and I were at a temple. There were geishas dancing. I was talking away to someone and acting like I knew it all. The person told me I needed to learn about *shoshin*. I asked our guide about it later that day and he explained it. *Shoshin* is a concept from Zen Buddhism that means beginner's mind. It's having an attitude of openness when studying, just as a beginner would."

"What does it have to do with me?" Robert asked.

"Well, many people come at things wearing what I call the *I-already-know-that* hat. Some of what I share, you may have already

17

heard before, but I'm hoping you'll take off the hat and keep a beginner's mindset."

"Sure, as long as you jump to Lesson 1, I'll practise show-shen," Robert promised.

Treb didn't correct Robert's pronunciation. He simply replied, "Okay, Lesson 1 it is. Lesson 1 is what I call the power of synchronicity."

"Synchronicity?"

"You might know it as coincidence," Treb explained. "But I have learned every so-called coincidence has meaning, whether small or big. I've heard others call synchronicities *meaningful coincidences*. For example, when I was sitting backstage one time before speaking, I got to talk to the legendary speaker Les Brown. Know him? He's been speaking for almost fifty years, and he talks with this booming voice. 'You gotta be hungry,' he says. Anyway, I asked him about …"

"You got to meet Les Brown?" Robert interrupted. "Of course, I know who he is!"

Treb nodded. "Yes, it was a humbling experience. And I asked him about synchronicity."

"What did he say?"

"As he put it, 'Synchronicity is God's way of staying anonymous.' I later found out others have described synchronicity that way, but hearing it from the legendary Les Brown gave me goosebumps. It still gives me goosebumps!" Treb said, showing Robert his arms.

Robert was awestruck. He'd been a fan of Les Brown for years. It must have been so cool to sit with that inspiring man for even five minutes.

"I have a favorite Les Brown insight. Do you?" Robert asked.

Treb leaned back in his seat, "I love when Les talks about the wealthiest place on Earth being the graveyard. He talked about it that day, in fact."

"The graveyard is the wealthiest place? I haven't heard that one. What does that even mean?"

"Well, Les told the crowd how one of his friends described the graveyard that way because it's the place where you'll find all the hopes and dreams that were never fulfilled—books that were never written, songs that were never sung, inventions that were never shared, cures that were never discovered, all because someone was too afraid to take the first step to carry out their dreams. Les says we should aim to live fully and die empty."

"Now I have goosebumps!"

Treb leaned forward again and continued. "So back to synchronicity. It's important to accept that not everything happens by accident. Some things—I would argue most—happen for a reason."

"Can you give me an example?"

"Sure. I'll tell you about meeting my wife, Gina. Actually, I met her when I was close to your age. Well, what I think your age is. Twenty-five?"

"Close," Robert said, even though Treb had guessed right.

Treb continued, "So I'd just gotten off another plane—I used to fly a lot. As usual, I was trying to rush through security to get on my next flight. A beautiful lady in a red dress happened to turn around after setting her luggage on the belt. In my rush, I bumped right into her. She dropped an envelope, and her passport and plane ticket fell out. But that wasn't what I noticed. What I noticed was a piece of paper with the name Diane on it. Diane is my mother's name. The name on her paper had nothing to do with my mother, but it gave me something to chat with Gina about later in the day. And, if you can believe it, it turned out Gina lived just up the road from me, but we'd never met!

Robert listened intently.

"It gets even crazier," Treb said. "She'd just purchased the flight that day. She'd been asked last minute to fill in for someone else on a big project her employer had landed. It was her first flight ever! And I was supposed to be on a different flight but had been bumped in a previous city due to issues with the plane. I mean, what are the odds of all that happening? I don't even think you could calculate them. Anyway, I was lucky enough to get her number that day. Thirty years later, we're still together."

"Come on," Robert said. "Coincidences happen all the time. I was just bumped from my last flight because of issues with the plane. Those things just happen."

"That's what I used to think. After I met Gina, though, I had another 'coincidence' happen right away. So I started to take notice."

"What was the other one?"

"Another time, I was on a plane, and I ended up sitting next to this man who looked wise beyond his years but also young for his age—or what appeared to be his age. I later found out he was in his late sixties, and yet he looked like someone in their late fifties, at most. We got to talking, and he said his name was James Redfield. I'd never heard that name before, so I didn't think much of it at first. But later in the flight, a middle-aged man came up to our seat. He leaned over and said to James, 'I'm so sorry to interrupt you, Sir, but I wanted to show you this. You're not going to believe it.' He held out the book he was reading, *The Celestine Prophecy* by James Redfield. I'd heard of the book but never read it.

"Anyway, James autographed the book, and then the man walked back to his own seat, blushing from meeting a celebrity. 'Wow, that's quite the coincidence that he was reading your book on this flight,' I said. 'Is it a coincidence?' he replied. 'I have that happen almost every day.' He then went on to tell me story after story about the synchronicities he'd experienced, even ones that helped *The Celestine* reach so many readers."

Treb took a sip from his bottle of water, while Robert looked on in expectation for the rest of the story.

Treb leaned back in his chair. "Now, James's first book, *The Celestine*, sold almost forty million copies. So you could argue it's not that surprising that someone on the plane was reading it. But it turns out people have stories of the book falling off the shelf in front of them when they're in a bookstore looking for a new book, or having three different people buy the book for them for their birthday at a time they needed the book's lessons the most.

"When I got home and told Gina about being on the flight with James, she told me *The Celestine Prophecy* was the first book on spirituality she'd read in college. She'd actually discovered it in a corner of the closet in her dorm room. It had to have been left behind when the previous student moved out.

"After that flight, I started believing in this thing called *synchronicity* and had a whole new appreciation for the idea of *coincidence*. I mean, even you and I sitting together, talking about this. What are the odds on that?" Treb asked.

Robert considered that he was supposed to be sitting next to an empty seat. "What did you learn about synchronicity?" he asked.

"One thing James said to me was how to bring more synchronicity into your life. He said what you notice, you get more of. So you have to really notice when synchronicity happens if you want to bring more of it into your life. I'm not a big writer, but from that idea, I started a journal and made bullet notes of each synchronicity that happened. I soon realized how often they were happening."

"Isn't that just like when you buy a car and then you start to see it more often? Isn't that coincidence?" Robert asked.

"I'll repeat what James said when I asked a similar question. Is it coincidence? Sure, you see the car more often, but there are no more of those cars out there than there were before you bought yours. It's just that you notice the car more because you're suddenly paying attention. This backs up the idea that what you notice, you get more of. The car part could be a way the universe tells you that you bought the right car.

"But imagine if you could create more important synchronicities, like the one I had with Gina?"

Robert was intrigued but still a bit skeptical. "You know, when I was at my previous job, which I never flew for, I got on a rare flight that was also a last-minute thing," Robert said. "When I boarded, the flight attendant offered me a different seat. I guess a kid had thrown up on my assigned one. The person I ended up sitting next to insisted on talking the entire time. I wanted to sleep but decided not to. He asked me what I did, and when I explained, he let me know about a job in his company—he thought I'd be a perfect fit. The man left the company a week later, but in that week, he interviewed me and hired me. And that's the job I'm doing now."

Treb nodded. "Synchronicity at work."

"Let me share another thing James taught me. He said when you keep seeing someone in a short amount of time, they likely have a message for you. I'll give you an example. A number of years ago, I was in a grocery store near my house. I happened to notice the nephew of a good friend at the store. I said hi to the kid and kept on shopping. Then, when I went to the store the next week, I saw the kid again. I was like, wow, that's interesting. I've never seen him here, and then I see him twice in just over a week. I just said hi again. But I knew somehow I should try and find out why I'd seen him twice. What message did he have? I didn't see him again at the store for maybe three weeks. But the next time, I told him I was friends with his uncle and asked if we could have a quick chat in the store's food court. He was a bit taken aback, but he indulged me.

"During our chat, he told me he'd just lost his job and was having little luck finding another one. He was also supporting his ailing mother, and was extremely worried about where his next paycheck would come from. I didn't know if this was the reason I'd been seeing him—to help him out—but when he told me what he did for a living, I was blown away. He was in the same industry. He was a driver, and we happened to need one. We hadn't even posted the job, as we figured we'd find someone through a referral.

"So I hired the kid—I guess he was twenty-one. And he did an awesome job. I kind of took him under my wing. He spent some time at my place for dinners. My goddaughter, also in her early twenties, even became smitten with him. They began dating, and now they're married and have a little girl. BUT, even bigger perhaps, a few years ago, my goddaughter was mugged outside their apartment. The young man saw what was happening and sprang to her rescue. He ended up getting stabbed, but he was okay. Had he not been a part of my life, my goddaughter might not still be with us today."

Robert didn't know what to say.

Treb continued. "So now I've told you about meeting Gina, meeting James, and finding out what message this kid had for me. What are the odds of having those three things happen? And they are only a small number of the synchronicities I've experienced. Taking notes helps me see them.

"I've also learned to listen to my intuition. If your intuition is leading you down a path, pay attention. You have more ability to sense the right path than you realize. In business, you might call it your 'gut feeling.' Whatever you call it, don't fight it. Listen to your gut, your intuition, to make decisions."

"So how does this help me succeed in business?" Robert asked.

Treb paused. "Look, I don't think the universe is trying to grow business necessarily, but I'd bet that more business deals, partnerships, and growth have been the result of synchronicities than any other thing. The biggest question is, are we paying attention?"

"Is that the only way to tap into this synchronicity stuff?" Robert asked.

"Well, some people get help from others—people who may be more tuned in."

"Psychics?" Robert asked.

"Yes, mediums. Astrologers. Every day, people benefit from such work. People use numbers to decide when to release projects. They use mediums to decide if they're on the right path.

"In fact, I was dragged to a medium by my friend years ago, just before I met one of my best friends. The medium told me I would meet someone with the first letter J, middle initial E, and last name starting with P. Soon after, I met Jean Isabelle Palmer."

"Wait," Robert interrupted. "That means her middle initial is I, not E."

"That what I thought too," Treb said with a nod. "But after a few weeks, my friend Jean told me that her aunt called her 'Esabelle' and had always argued that her middle name was Esabelle with an E because she was named after her aunt Esabelle with an E."

"Wow," Robert said.

"Yes, when you note these things, you see more of them. A medium also told me that she could see me on my twenty-sixth birthday in Sedona, Arizona, on horseback. I was with the person she said I'd meet with the letter G, and we were overlooking the sunset. I had just started dating Gina, so I assumed she meant her. I'd never even heard of Sedona."

"I've never heard of it either."

"It's a beautiful place surrounded by red rock and sand. They say there's powerful energy there. They have this amazing buddha statue you can find if you walk through the trees. Anyway, since I hadn't heard of the place, I thought there was no way I'd be going in a few years. I never told Gina about the medium either. But when Gina later planned a surprise vacation for my twenty-sixth birthday, guess where it was?"

"No way," Robert replied.

"Yes, Sedona. And what did she plan for my special day? Horseback riding!"

"Are you making this up?" Robert asked.

"I know. It sounds crazy. If I were you, I'm not even sure I'd believe it. But once I started noticing synchronicities and acting on them, my life changed."

"Is that the only way to attract synchronicities?"

"No," Treb said. "Once you start living more spiritually, you experience more. The universe rewards those who engage in what the universe delivers. So walking in nature, meditating, loving others, and reading can help."

"Well, I read," Robert said. "But what should I be reading?"

"There are many great books. *The Celestine Prophecy. Think and Grow Rich. The Science of Getting Rich.*"

"I like the sound of those last two—especially the getting rich part," Robert said.

"Those two books are about creating abundance and material wealth, but they're also about becoming a richer person."

"So they take the fun out of getting rich then?" Robert joked.

Treb laughed. "Another way to enjoy synchronicity is to be more playful. Oh, and you have to set clear intentions."

"You mean like that manifesting stuff I hear people talk about?" Robert asked.

"Yes, that manifesting stuff. Synchronicity and manifestation and abundance all go hand in hand. So it helps to jot down what you want and then watch the synchronicities happen. Besides, even if you don't get everything you want, isn't life more fun when you play with it a little? Even if you don't get everything, you'll still get more than if you aren't clear."

"Sounds like pseudo-science to me," Robert said. "And I won't always get what I want?"

"Think of the lines from that Stones song about not getting what you want but getting what you need. You need to be flexible. The universe delivers what you need, maybe not exactly what you ask for. The universe might save you from a job you think you want but with a horrible boss—and instead give you a job you didn't know you wanted. But it's the job of your dreams."

"I've had situations like that," Robert said. "Sometimes we lose a deal and think it's the end of the world, only to end up with a better contract or customer because we lost that initial deal."

"It's exactly like that," Treb agreed. "One thing I forgot. If you want to attract more positive things and synchronicities, you also need to stop *stinking thinking*."

"Stinking thinking?" Robert asked.

"Yes. *Stinking thinking* is something the late great Zig Ziglar often talked about. The term was coined by a psychologist, Albert Ellis. It describes our tendency to always think negative thoughts."

"Zig Ziglar?"

"He was an iconic speaker from the South. He got his start selling pots and pans and Bibles door to door."

"What?" Robert said.

"That's right—pots and pans and Bibles. Aren't you glad you weren't in sales in the fifties?"

"I am now," Robert replied. Robert didn't admit it to Treb, but he knew he had many *stinking thinking* moments. "That's a lot to remember for Lesson 1," he said.

"Agreed," Treb said. "All I'm saying is to try a few of the steps. You can judge the results for yourself."

Actions for Lesson 1:
Embrace the power of synchronicity.

1. Start a synchronicity journal and make notes of each synchronicity that happens.
2. When you see someone more than once in a short amount of time, find out what message they have for you.
3. When your intuition speaks, take its advice.
4. Walk in nature, meditate, read, and love others.
5. Be more playful with the universe.
6. Eliminate stinking thinking.

Chapter 5:
THE SCAR

"Now, let's talk about Lesson 2," Treb said.

"Actually," Robert interrupted, "I have to go to the bathroom."

Treb got up from his seat to let Robert pass by, and Robert made his way to the front of the plane. On his way, he approached another passenger who was stretching his legs out into the aisle. "Do you mind?" Robert said. "I'm trying to get to the bathroom."

The man moved his legs. When he thought Robert was out of earshot, the man said, "What's that guy's problem?"

When Robert returned, Treb again stood up to let Robert back into their row. As Robert walked past Treb, he noticed a scar on Treb's left arm.

"How did you get that?"

"This?" Treb said, looking down at his scar. "A bar fight ten years ago."

"Really?"

"Well, sort of. I was in Liverpool, England. Taking in a bunch of Beatles stuff. I even had the chance to play at the Cavern Club, where the Beatles played."

"You played what?"

"I play guitar and sing. I write music," Treb explained. "I picked it up like ten years ago."

"I have always wanted to play guitar. Women love that!" Robert said. "I could never play, though. I'm tone deaf."

"You'd be surprised what's possible when you put in the hours."

Robert shrugged.

"Anyway, after my set at the Cavern Club, a fight broke out," Treb continued. "I didn't start it and wasn't really involved, but I got stabbed with a piece of glass. I guess I'll never forget my Beatles trip!" he said, looking back down at his scar. Then he looked down at his forearm at a tattoo located just above the Om. "I got this tattoo on that trip as well."

"That's a Beatle, isn't it?" Robert asked.

"John Lennon. I kind of became obsessed with the Beatles like twenty years back."

"Well, I guess we do have one thing in common. I have a similar tattoo," Robert said, pointing to Treb's Om tattoo under the one of John Lennon.

"So, Lesson 2?" Robert asked.

"Yes, Lesson 2. What if the journey is really the destination?"

"That sounds like a riddle," Robert said.

"Not really. I've spent a lot of time with peak performers. And I've discovered something interesting that top performers seem to go through but don't really talk about."

"What?" Robert asked.

"I have a story that will explain it really well."

"Surprise, surprise."

Treb smiled.

"I'm just kidding," Robert said. "Go ahead."

"A successful business lady once told me how a friend of her husband's had sold his business for hundreds of millions. His first purchase after the sale was a home worth eighty million. When the lady and her husband went over to visit this friend, they found him on this huge back deck. And guess what he was doing? He was looking through a magazine at other luxury homes. He'd discovered a home worth ninety-five million, and wondered if he'd be happier there. Here this man was living in this elaborate mansion, wondering if he would be happier in a bigger home."

"What's the point?" Robert asked.

"The point is he wasn't enjoying the journey. I see it all the time. People set out to write a book. They work on the book for months, sometimes years, and all they talk about is when the book will be out. 'When the book is out, it'll be awesome. I'll be happy once the book is out. This book is going to change everything.' I also see it in the work world. People say, 'When I retire, then I'll be happy.' But when they retire, some of these people pass away weeks later. How sad that they never truly lived their lives while they had them. They waited for some magical moment in the future."

"Perhaps they're miserable at their jobs," Robert said. "It's hard to live fully when you hate your job. And it's not like they can just leave a job that pays the bills. People need security."

"But do they have security?" Treb replied. "I would argue there's no such thing as job security anymore. Running your own business is just as secure as working for someone else. Companies downsize daily.

I don't advocate quitting your job without having something to go to. I'm just saying that *security* is a myth. And does it make sense to stay in a job that makes you miserable, when life is short?"

"I guess not."

"To me, part of enjoying the journey is enjoying your work," Treb said. "If you don't enjoy what you do, doesn't it make sense to look for something else? As long as you can pay your bills, doesn't it make sense to do something you like?"

"So what's the real lesson?"

"I was talking about people writing books. Too often, they aren't enjoying the process of actually writing. They're focused on holding the completed book in their hands. Then, I see many of those same people holding that final book and wondering what's next. They aren't enjoying the journey. Actually, they're not even enjoying the destination. They're already looking for the next thing.

"So Lesson 2 is all about enjoying the journey AND the destination. Many top leaders don't—they don't enjoy each moment. No one really talks about it either. But I think the more open we can be, the better we can deal with it."

"What can we do about it?" Robert asked.

"Find ways to become more present, to live in the moment. If we go back to the book example, it could mean picking a writing spot you love. Like writing in nature or overlooking the water. I don't naturally love writing, but I have learned to enjoy the process. For me, it's often about the energy of the place I'm writing in."

"The energy of the place?"

"Yes. When I write, I have this place I go to. It's a little town called Sitges, in Spain. They have amazing architecture and beaches. I sit on a bench in front of the beach in this historic town and write. I even know the locals now. Every now and then, someone from the local gelato store will bring me out some coco gelato. I'm gluten-free, and they know I get hungry while writing!"

"You're gluten-free? Are you also a vegan? Do you drink soy lattes?!" Robert asked, a hint of sarcasm in his voice.

"Did I hit a nerve?" Treb asked.

"Sorry—I just get tired of people being so trendy with how they eat."

"I wish! I'm not gluten-free by choice. If I have gluten, it will cause a major flare up. Last time I had it, I was in pain for over a week."

"I guess that's different," Robert said.

"Anyway, if you enjoy writing in a certain place, do that. If you don't enjoy writing, create an outline of what you'd like to say, get your ideas on paper, hire a ghostwriter to do the writing you don't really love, and do something else.

"Being in the moment can also mean taking time to stand in nature, learning to breathe consciously, sitting in silence, meditating, or practising yoga. Performing random acts of kindness is another way. *The Power of Now* says every minute you spend worrying about the future or regretting the past is a minute lost, because, really, all you have is now."

"Wait a minute," Robert interrupted. "I don't get how you can enjoy the journey by doing yoga? Or meditation? How does this help put money in your pocket?"

"It's not just about money. I'm saying if you embrace synchronicity, meditation, spirituality, and yoga, you'll become the type of person who draws in more abundance. You'll have more great moments. You'll become richer in money and character. But I'll get to some practical stuff."

Just then, the flight attendant appeared back at their row. She looked at Robert and asked, "Is there anything I can get you?"

"Sure, I'll have another scotch on the rocks, please."

"I'll get right on it," she said, before proceeding to the cart, grabbing a glass, and pouring the drink.

When she returned and handed Robert his scotch, Treb piped up. "Nothing for me, thanks." But the flight attendant was already headed down the aisle. Treb looked at Robert. "I guess if you're not supposed to be in first class, they don't look at you the same way," he said.

Robert tipped his glass to Treb. "Let's get to Lesson 3. I want to get to the practical stuff. I can get my head around practical."

Action for Lesson 2:
Enjoy the journey and the destination.

1. Find ways to be in the now. Embrace meditation, spirituality, yoga, and random acts of kindness.

Chapter 6:

THE PRACTICAL LESSON

Treb didn't seem in any rush to get to Lesson 3.

"Let me share one more way to enjoy the journey and improve your energy," he told Robert. "It's a strategy to get into your zone any time you want."

Robert's eyes widened. "That's a tall order."

"It's something I discovered in the strangest way. I call it the perfect moment. Let me set the stage. Gina and I had purchased tickets for a Buddy Guy show."

"Buddy Guy? The old blues dude?" Robert asked.

"Yes, exactly. We saw him at Massey Hall in Toronto, Canada. The show was brilliant. The guy was eighty-five, and he tore down the house. Anyway, while he was playing a guitar solo, I looked over at Gina and took a mental screenshot. This was my perfect moment. An unforgettable guitar solo, while sitting next to my favorite person in the world.

"I realized I could bring myself to a certain energy, or zone, simply by revisiting that perfect moment. Someone else might think of their wedding, the birth of a child, a concert, a sunset. If you can recall a perfect moment, you can change your energy."

"How can I use this for business?" Robert asked.

"Well, think about how much better you'd perform in meetings or sales calls if you visualized a perfect moment just before you entered the meeting or client's office. It works both ways. If you're worried about being rejected or if you're thinking of the worst outcome, odds are you won't have your best meeting. You can influence the outcome of your day by choosing to transport yourself to a perfect moment."

"I like that idea," Robert said. "I'm going to try it. So what's Lesson 3?" Robert asked.

But before Treb could speak, Robert continued. "Wait. I think what you just shared—about putting yourself into your zone—I think I learned that at a Tony Robbins event. Robert thought for a minute. "Actually it was a real estate event, the Learning Annex. Tony was one of the speakers. He got us to look at the person on our right and sell them a pen, then look at the person on our left and sell them a pen. He told us to think of the best moment of our life when we sold to the right and the worst when we sold to the left. When we pictured our worst day, we were slumped over, talked lower, and seemed depressed. When we pictured our best day, we had our chests out, spoke loudly, and smiled. I thought it was a cool exercise, but I was so focused on selling the pen. I didn't realize I could use it in my daily life, that I could create my energy through visualization."

"That's exactly what he was teaching you," Treb said.

"Lesson 3?" Robert asked.

"I guess you still need practice living in the moment," Treb said with a laugh. "So, Lesson 3 I learned by burning myself out. It was shortly after I'd met Gina. I was working most evenings and some weekends. I thought she'd respect my work ethic. So if a client wanted me to fly to their location or work extra hours, I would say yes. I thought the best way to succeed was saying yes to everyone and everything, then figuring out how to do it later. The result, of course, was burnout. It hurt my relationship with Gina, and I realized I was saying yes too much.

"That's when I discovered the power of no. This is Lesson 3. Say no to all the things that won't move the needle in your life and career, so you can say yes to the things that will.

"I learned this lesson from necessity. Once I was burned out, I couldn't say yes, even if I wanted to. So I had to start saying no. It wasn't easy for someone like me, who thought yes was the way to success."

"I admit, I say yes a lot—if the situation will benefit me," Robert said.

"Most people do," Treb said. "But I made *no* my new mantra."

Action for Lesson 3:
Make 'no' a new mantra.

1. Say no to the many things that will not move the needle in your work or life, so you can say yes to the few things that do.

Chapter 7:
THE MISSION

"**S**o when you figured out how to say no, how did you figure out what to say no to?" Robert asked.

"I had to learn what a *yes* was, versus what a *no* was. If you have a strong mission statement, you can start to tell them apart."

"A mission statement? Isn't that just for companies?"

"That's the issue," Treb said. "Most great companies have a powerful mission statement, but few individuals do. Having a strong mission statement helps you create clarity."

"Can you give me an example?"

"Sure, I'll tell you mine. It's DEMI. Like Demi Moore. That is, to Donate, Entertain, Motivate, and Inspire. I actually learned it from a hairstylist during a conference I was facilitating. I had everyone come up with mission statements. When the hairstylist shared hers, I said, 'That's better than mine. Mine doesn't have an acronym. Do you mind if I steal it?' The rest is history.

"If what I'm being asked to do isn't covering some of those areas—allowing me to donate, entertain, motivate, or inspire—it's an easy NO. If it involves at least two or more of those areas, it's an easy YES. It's as simple as that. It makes life so much easier."

"That's truly powerful," Robert said. "I'll have to come up with my own."

"It'll change everything; I promise."

"But people don't like hearing *no*," Robert said. "How do you say *no* without burning bridges?"

"Well, when people ask for help, they're often looking for an instant answer. Let's say someone asks you to help them move. Maybe you have a bad back, but you say yes because you feel obligated. Instead, what if you asked for some time? You might say you need a day to check with your partner or spouse, to see if something is planned for that day. You ask if you can reply about the moving the next day. You let them know that if you can't help, you will try to find someone who can. How can someone get mad at you for making sure you're not spoiling plans with someone else, asking for time to consider, and offering to suggest someone who can help if you can't? I've done this many times, and I can't think of one time when the other person was upset. Often, by the time I get back to them, they've already found a solution and don't need my help after all."

"I have to admit, that is very practical," Robert said.

"And here's something else that is very practical, around feeding your mind."

"What's that?"

"Creating your own learning plan."

"A learning plan?" Robert asked.

"Yes. You could listen to a podcast three days a week, read twenty minutes a day, or attend a live conference once a month. It doesn't have to be super structured, but it should give you a learning approach that helps you grow. That helps you carry out your mission statement. Speaker Brian Tracy once said that if you listen to the right stuff while driving to and from work, you could have the equivalent of a university degree after just a couple of years. He called it a mobile library."

"A mobile library? I like that. It does sound practical."

"Well, if you like that idea, let me tell you about the 'Hour of Power.' I was on a retreat years ago in Costa Rica, and one of the speakers talked on and on about his 'Hour of Power.' He didn't explain what it was. He simply kept telling us it was responsible for most of his success. Finally, I cornered him and convinced him to tell me about it.

"It was actually quite simple. Essentially, his hour of power revolved around three things he did as soon as he woke up every day. He would spend twenty minutes learning something, twenty minutes meditating, and twenty minutes exercising. Every day, he was feeding his mind, spirit, and body."

"And you do this every day?"

"Yes, it's another thing that changed everything for me. Now, I would tell anyone who tries it not to start with the full hour. Just do five to ten minutes of each. Five minutes of each activity won't seem like a massive commitment, so it's easier to succeed."

"You know, Treb, you should have started with this one," Robert said. "I can see why it works!"

"Maybe I thought that if I started with this one, you might not listen to the others."

Treb and Robert started laughing.

"You know, you're probably right," Robert said.

With that, Treb stood up and said, "Now, I have to go to the bathroom."

Robert thought about the things Treb had shared. He wondered if he might need to make changes in his life if he wanted to experience richness, material or personal. As he considered some of the changes he could make, he hardly noticed that Treb had returned and was getting seated next to him.

"So, Lesson 4?" Treb asked, as he sat into his seat.

Actions for Lesson 3 (continued):
Make 'no' a new mantra.

1. Write your own personal mission statement.
2. Create your own learning plan.

Chapter 8:

THE MAYFLY

"There's a great quote in *The Alchemist,* by Paulo Coelho," Treb said.

"*The Alchemist*?"

"Have you read it?" Treb asked.

"No," Robert replied.

"Well, you should add it to your list. There's a great quote in the book that goes something along the lines of, 'When each day is the same as the next, it's because people fail to recognize the good things that happen in their lives every day that the sun rises.' There's also another great quote by Henry David Thoreau."

"I know who he is," Robert said. "I heard about him in high school."

Treb continued, "Thoreau said, 'The mass of men lead lives of quiet desperation.' These quotes really relate to Lesson 4. It's about how you're living your life and whether it brings you happiness. Let me ask you a question. Did you know the mayfly only lives twenty-four hours?"

"Only twenty-four hours? And what's a mayfly?"

"It's a winged insect. And yes, just twenty-four hours. That's the male. The female only lives five to ten minutes."

"Wow. That's crazy."

"Agreed. But it raises an interesting point. If this was your last day on Earth, what would you do?"

Robert began to answer. "Hmmm. I'd probably call my mother. Maybe I'd call my ex-girlfriend who cheated on me and tell her I forgive her. I might buy a cat. My life is too busy for a dog, but it would be great to have a pet. I'd start eating better …"

"On your last day?" Treb interjected. "That's interesting."

"I'd also listen to my favorite records on the record player I bought some time ago and haven't even plugged in. Or maybe I'd start learning guitar. Girls love guitars."

"So why aren't you doing these things now?"

"Great question. I guess we never believe it will be our last day."

"I almost had a last day," Treb confessed. "In fact, when I got stabbed in Liverpool, that could have been my last day, but we had an even closer call!"

"We?"

"Gina and I," Treb explained. "We were exploring Los Angeles, near Hollywood. Someone ran past us and screamed, 'Earthquake!' I hadn't even felt anything yet."

"Maybe he was a psychic," Robert joked. "Or maybe a tourist."

"Maybe," Treb replied. "Before we could react, I heard something above us. I looked up to see a piece of a building falling. I grabbed Gina and pulled her out of the way. We both fell on the sidewalk, just inches away from where the piece of building had crashed to the ground."

"That is a close call," Robert said. "I guess that would have a person thinking about how they were living their life."

"It did, for both of us."

Treb and Robert sat in silence for a minute.

Finally, Treb spoke. "So, in keeping with Coelho's quote from *The Alchemist*, the first part of Lesson 4 is noting things to be grateful for. For example, did you know that if you work at a fast-food restaurant in North America, you're richer than half the world?"

"No."

"It's true. But how many people take that for granted? So the first step is to simply recognize all the good in your life and the blessing you have just to be above ground. A journal could be one way to do that."

"What kind of journal?"

"It doesn't matter. The best journal is one you actually use to note the good things in your life."

"The second part of Lesson 4 is to ask yourself the question I just asked you: how would you live your last day? Ask that question and write down the answer. Then, start living that way now. There's a great quote credited to Gandhi, something like, 'Live every day like you could die tomorrow, but plan like you could live forever.'"

"You like quotes, don't you?" Robert said.

"Yes. I like that quotes can change the way we think and act. Now, back to the living every day like it could be your last. You have to plan for the future, but asking the question helps you understand what makes a great day for you and live accordingly. You could simply make notes about your ideal day and then take action on the first thing on the list. Once you've done that, then move to the second, and so on. Don't take on too much at once. But imagine if everyone lived this way?"

"The world would look a lot different, that's for sure," Robert said. "So, if I understand correctly, the first part of Lesson 4 is to be grateful for what you have, and for the fact you're still here. The second part is to figure out your best day and aim to live that way, every day. How does this make you rich?"

"Well, we've talked about being richer personally and professionally. This will make you richer in both ways. Your gratitude raises your vibration and positive energy. When you're operating at a higher vibration, you attract more abundance."

"Whoa. That's over my head. It sounds like the stuff they said in that *Secret* movie."

"It is that kind of stuff," Treb said. "You don't have to know *why* it works really, just that it does. Look at the people in *The Secret*. Bob Proctor, for example. He was eighty-five when I spoke with him, and he had the energy of a twenty-five-year-old. He was also rich too! I know that's the part that interests you.

"Lisa Nichols is also in it. She's created a following that has allowed her to impact millions of lives through her Motivating the Masses brand. John Assaraf. He's sixty, but he's also got the energy of a much younger man—and massive abundance.

"And Jack Canfield, who helped create the billion-dollar Chicken Soup brand. Jack and his writing partner, the co-creator Mark Victor Hansen, were turned down over 140 times by publishers who said no one would buy the book. Since then, they've sold over 600 million books. They've impacted millions of lives. And they didn't start with Chicken Soup until their late forties!

"But the main point is this. Proctor, Nichols, Assaraf, and Canfield have all practised what they shared in *The Secret*. Look at the results. They've figured out how to raise their vibration and operate at a higher level. Their successes have continued long past when they were in *The Secret*."

"I like results," Robert said. "Is there anything else to Lesson 4?"

"Yes. We've chatted about being grateful and making sure you're living every day to the fullest. We also need to talk about planning. I think it was Warren Buffett who talked about this. Or maybe Robin Sharma. Or maybe both. Either way, they spoke about figuring out what you'd like your life to look like when you're eighty and then reverse-engineering it by asking what you need to do between now and then to have that life. For instance, what do you have to do this year, then next year. Then you have a game plan."

"That's a cool concept," Robert said.

"It just gives you so much clarity," Treb agreed. "The next step is to write your obituary."

"What?" asked Robert, a look of shock on his face.

"You heard me—write your obituary."

"Isn't that super morbid?"

"I've had so many people respond that way during lectures when I get them to break out and work on their obituaries. Funny enough, the same people who kick up the biggest fuss are the ones who are disappointed when I tell them it's time to put down the pen. I've had people, months after a lecture, reach out and tell me they kept writing until they had eighteen pages about what they'd like people to know about them after they're gone."

"I can't believe I'm even considering doing that," Robert said. "But I guess I have nothing to lose. I can always put the pen down. What made you decide to write your obituary?"

"That day in Los Angeles. I realized I still hadn't lived up to my potential. I thought about what I wanted my life to look like by the time it was my last day. If a falling piece of a building could end it all that easily, maybe it was time to make sure I didn't have any regrets."

"So Lesson 4 is all about how you're living your life now and how you should live your life?"

"Essentially, yes. Should we go to Lesson 5?" Treb asked.

"Actually, before you do, I have a question," Robert said.

"Sure, shoot."

"Well, we were talking about that *Secret* movie."

"It was also a book," Treb added.

"Okay, so the book, the movie. It kind of took the world by storm. It was on Oprah. Everyone seemed to be talking about it. Almost every friend of mind was talking about how they were going to visualize themselves rich. Few of them did. If this stuff works, what gives? Why didn't it work?"

"It's a valid question. It did change a lot of lives. There's a thing called Mind Movies, which is like a video vision board. It was created by Natalie and Glen Ledwell. They built a million-dollar brand and have reached millions of people based on the teachings in *The Secret*. But I think *The Secret* left out some elements, I think mostly due to lack of time. I've talked to a lot of people who watched *The Secret* who didn't know the actions they should take. *The Secret* focused mostly on the Law of Attraction but didn't really cover the Law of Action. And it's just as important. I think I can sum it up by sharing a chat I had with Lisa Nichols."

"You met Lisa Nichols?"

"Yes, I was working on a project and had the chance to interview her. One of the things she told me summed up the importance of action. She said you can have the greatest vision board in the world hanging on your living room wall. You can look at it ten times a day and believe those things will happen, but if all you do is sit on the couch watching TV, all you'll have to show for it is a lump in the couch."

"So it was the action part that people struggled with?"

"It wasn't only that. It was also a matter of people saying they were going to attract something they didn't truly believe was possible. You know, saying 'I'm a millionaire' when they were struggling to pay the bills. If you can't truly get in the space of feeling like you're a millionaire, your subconscious mind will know the difference and act accordingly.

"There's a great book by a Law of Attraction pioneer named Neville. It's called *At Your Command.* The book says you really have to feel and believe with every ounce of your being that you've already attracted whatever you want to manifest. That isn't easy. I heard a talk one time by someone named Cappi …. I can't remember her last name. Anyway, I saw her speak in Hawaii. I had taken a lecture, mostly for the trip to Hawaii. The event was in Honolulu, and I'd brought Gina with me. We came off the long flight, and that morning, we were at the Hawaii Convention Center. I really just wanted some rest. Gina reminded me, though, how much more impact I would have on the audience the following day if I'd spent some time watching the other speakers and could comment on some of the things they said."

"Sounds like a wise woman," Robert said.

"She is," Treb agreed.

He continued with his story. "So I went to the venue and caught the talk by this Cappi person. Pidwell. That's her last name. Cappi Pidwell talked about how many years she'd spent helping people manifest, and she changed the way I understood the Law of Attraction. She said even though the Law of Attraction always works, many people get in their own way because they don't truly believe what they are telling themselves. She said it's because the conscious mind produces only five percent of our thoughts. The subconscious is responsible for ninety-five percent. So even if you are saying something over and over at a conscious level, when you don't believe it on an unconscious level, it's an obstacle. Essentially, what you're saying out loud is incongruent with what your subconscious mind 'knows' to be true."

"So how can you fool your subconscious mind?"

"Cappi says you need to say something you can truly believe. Instead of saying 'I am a millionaire,' she says ask yourself what you believe. If you believe it will take ten years to make a million dollars, it will be hard for you to make ten million in twelve months. In other words, you need to change your beliefs. To do that, she suggests writing down something like 'I'm beginning to believe that _____ is possible.' This way, you can start to believe something is possible rather than trying to convince yourself it's already happened."

"That makes so much sense," Robert admitted.

"Yes. I went from someone who was struggling with this Law of Attraction idea and missing the action plan to understanding that I was manifesting something I could imagine being possible."

Actions for Lesson 4:
Live each day like it's your last (but plan like it's not).

1. Consider starting a gratitude journal.
2. Write about your perfect day. Try to live accordingly.
3. Imagine your desired future and reverse-engineer it to come up with a game plan.

Chapter 9:
THE FEAR

"So what's Lesson 5?" Robert asked.

"Let me start with another story. When Gina and I got our first pets together, we got two kittens. They were in this house, along with about twenty-five other kittens. The people were selling them for $100 each. Gina fell in love with this gray, long-haired cat. The sellers convinced us we should also take its brother, a black, longhaired cat.

"After we left, we talked about all those kittens in one small space; it really wasn't the best living conditions. We found out later from our vet that the kittens were older than we were told. We also realized our two kittens had issues with nervousness. If you walked toward the black cat, he ran. The gray cat ducked her head when you went to pet her. These issues never really went away. We gave them a great home, and they loved us, but they were still nervous all the time. Even when they were twelve years old, they would run to hide when visitors came over. Nothing ever happened to them under our watch. And yet, they lived in fear every day."

"That's kind of sad, isn't it?"

"It is. But isn't that how most people live? They're afraid of what may happen. They make decisions based on fear. And yet, what they fear rarely happens. How sad is that? I heard this great quote by Michael J. Fox: 'If you have one foot in yesterday and one foot in tomorrow, you're peeing all over today.' Now, I'm not saying you shouldn't think about the future. But we shouldn't worry so much about what happened yesterday or what might happen tomorrow. That's how our cats lived. They feared what might happen."

"So what do you propose?"

"If you start to worry, write down the answer to this question: Will the thing I'm worrying about now matter in a year, let alone five or ten? In almost every case, except perhaps the death of a family member, you'd forget about the thing in a year's time. So why worry about it now?"

The flight attendant came back to their row and interrupted the conversation. "Beef or veggies?" she asked.

"Sorry, what's that?" Robert replied.

"Beef or veggies?" she repeated. "We have beef or veggie wraps for lunch."

"Beef," Robert said.

"None for me, thanks," Treb replied.

With that, the flight attendant scurried off. She came back with two beef wrap halves stacked on a small white plate.

"Back to worries," Robert said, looking at Treb while he picked up one of the wraps. "Can you give me an example?"

"What about relationships?" Treb asked. I mean, how many people go through a breakup and think they'll never experience love again. Six months later, they're in a new relationship—wondering why they stayed with the other person so long.

"Let me give you another example. Someone is a hypochondriac. Any time they read about a disease, they think they have it. They even start developing symptoms. They're always worried they're sick or dying with something they don't even have."

"That's a terrible way to live," Robert said.

"Definitely. I was just reading *How to Stop Worrying and Start Living* by Dale Carnegie. He shares story after story of people who literally worried themselves sick. In some cases, they couldn't get out of bed. But what was making them sick was the worry itself.

"We do it with small things too. A kid worries he won't get the toy when he gets to the store, so he stresses about it all the way there. An adult worries about getting called for jury duty because his neighbor did. He doesn't get called, and so he puts all this energy into something that never happens."

"I never thought about it like that. So Lesson 5 is like the earlier one about living in the present?"

"Actually, no. It's about what I consider to be one of the most powerful words in the English language."

"What's the word?" Robert asked.

"*Mindset.*"

"Mindset?"

"Yes, *mindset* is everything. Is the glass half-full? Half-empty? Or can you fill that glass yourself? Whatever you believe affects your life. If you believe something bad will happen or you can't succeed, you will likely be right. If you believe something good will happen or you will succeed, you will likely be right."

"Can we change our mindset?" Robert asked.

"Of course. For one, we can increase our positive energy. We can read the right stuff, listen to the right stuff, and watch the right stuff. Feeding our mind positive things can start to change our mindset. Zig Ziglar once told me he'd only read things that helped him improve, personally or professionally. It works both ways too. I often tell people to take a news detox—or at least stop taking in so much of it. When you think of it, most of the news we hear or see is negative.

"We also need to watch what we say. What we think and what we say create our reality. You can't always be talking negatively and expect to have positive outcomes. So those are great starts."

"Great starts?" Robert asked.

"Yes, well, there are other ways to improve your mindset. In *The Celestine Prophecy,* James Redfield talks about increasing your energy while sitting in stillness."

"That sounds like meditation."

"It is meditation. Combine it with regular yoga practice, and you've got yourself some mindset game changers."

"Yoga? Meditation?" Robert asked. "I can't see myself sitting cross-legged on top of a mountain doing things like—what is it called—upward cat?"

"Downward dog," Treb said with a laugh. "When I was your age, I couldn't imagine it either. Gina convinced me to give a yoga class a try. At the end, we'd lie in this pose they call *savasana*. It's basically lying on the ground in silence. You're kind of lying like you're dead."

"Dead?"

"Yes, some people call it the corpse pose."

"Sounds kind of morbid!"

"The idea is to do nothing. A corpse is perfectly still. The mind is still too—no expectations, no thinking about the things to do later. After a few classes, I noticed how relaxing the pose was. The instructor said this was what meditation was like. I was sold."

"So you now sit cross-legged on mountains?"

"That's a common misconception about meditation, I think. That you have to do it a certain way. I love what Davidji says."

"Who's Davidji?"

"A meditation guru. He used to work for Deepak Chopra. He says meditation wasn't designed to have so many rules. You can meditate lying down. You can meditate for seventeen seconds."

"Lying down I could do," Robert said. "That seems more comfortable."

"We also talked about gratitude. That helps improve our mindset too."

"So we have mindset covered then?"

"Almost," Treb said. "If I can say one more thing, it's to remember that a new mindset means jumping outside of your comfort zone."

"I've jumped out of a plane!" Robert said. "That kind of thing?"

"Yes, that kind of thing. If you're scared of heights, jumping out of a plane will help you realize you can do things you might otherwise think aren't possible. In sales, it might mean calling a bigger company. For me, it was performing stand-up."

"You've performed stand-up comedy?" Robert asked. "Unbelievable!"

"The goal is to live fully," Treb said with a smile.

"You've done a lot."

"And a lot of it has been outside my comfort zone, like performing stand-up comedy on stage. For other people, it could be asking someone on a date. Writing a book. Cooking supper for the family. If we don't do new things, are we really living?"

"I guess it depends what the things are."

"Yes, that's a great point," Treb said. "I'm not talking about stuff that's illegal or hurtful. I mean stuff we want to do but don't because it's uncomfortable. There's a great quote by Neale Donald Walsch that says, 'Life begins at the end of your comfort zone.'"

"Who is Neale Donald ... what was the last name?"

"Neale Donald Walsch. He wrote *Conversations with God: An Uncommon Dialogue*."

"Never heard of it," Robert said. "So how do we get outside our comfort zone?"

"Decide we want to. And then make a plan. Before I performed stand-up on stage, I read books. I went to workshops. I watched comedy shows and took notes on what jokes worked. I even took out a local comic for dinner so I could pick his brain."

"Why not just dive right in?"

"If it's something you're afraid of, it will be tough to tackle. It's easier to break it down into smaller steps, take the steps, and reward yourself. Then the big step, like performing stand-up on stage, won't seem so big."

"Where did you learn all of this stuff?" Robert asked.

"Well, I've learned a lot from reading and the people I meet. Also from experience and travel. I travel a lot. When I'm on the road, I pay attention to what people are reading. I often strike up conversations—I'm sure that doesn't surprise you! Anyway, the people who are reading things that will improve their mindset, I find they're the more positive."

Just then, the flight attendant returned. "Can I take that out of your way, Mr. Stapleton?" she asked. Robert had finished most of the wrap.

"Sure," Robert said, handing over the plate.

Treb continued. "The great news is, it doesn't matter where you are now with life. You always get a do-over."

"It's never too late?" Robert asked.

"It's never too late," Treb assured.

Actions for Lesson 5:
Mindset is everything.

1. Find ways to increase your positive energy. Try meditation.
2. Ask yourself if the thing that you are worrying about will matter in five or ten years.
3. Be mindful of your words and thoughts. Keep them positive.
4. Take a news detox.
5. Jump outside of your comfort zone.

Chapter 10:

YOUR CIRCLE

"I have an exercise for you," Treb said.

"An exercise? Like push-ups?" Robert asked. "I just ate!"

"Not a physical exercise. Something with pen and a paper, an exercise I created. At the time, I was struggling with anxiety. It was impacting my personal and professional life. I knew I was reading and feeding my mind with positive things. But I wondered how I was being affected by the people around me. So I took out a piece of paper and a pen and started writing down names of the people I spent time with."

"And what did you find?" Robert asked.

"I'm getting there, my impatient friend," Treb said with a smile. "After I put down the names of people I spent time with, I put a plus sign beside the ones who brought positive energy to my life. I put a minus sign beside the ones who brought negative energy. Then I started a new piece of paper and drew a line down the centre. I put the positive names on one side and the negative ones on the other. Suddenly, I could see the imbalance."

"What was the imbalance?" Robert asked.

"I was spending most of my time with negative people," Treb explained. "I had three positive and sixteen negative. This included some of my family, friends, people I worked with, suppliers. I'm not saying they were all extremely negative, but many were bringing more negative energy, even just gossiping, than positive energy."

"Wow! You think you'd notice that."

"You would think so," Treb agreed. "But I hadn't. Perhaps just because I was busy. Things were on autopilot. I mean, here I was lecturing people that they should go on a news detox to remove negative energy from their lives, and yet I had so much negative energy in my own life! So Lesson 6 is about the importance of who you surround yourself with."

"It's really that important?" Robert asked.

"In some ways, it's everything."

"Well, what did you do? Did you *fire* everyone from your life?"

"Of course, it's not that easy," Treb replied. "For example, Gina was definitely on the positive side. But my mother, well, she was slightly on the negative side."

"My mother is kind of negative too," Robert said. "I can totally relate."

"My mother brought me into this world. I'm also sure she could take me out!" Treb said with a laugh. "And I love my mother. She made so many sacrifices for me. I could never remove her from my life."

"I feel the same. I couldn't remove my mother either," Robert agreed. "What did you do?"

"I didn't fire everyone. I just went through the list. I figured out who to remove, who to spend less time with, and how I could add more positive people to my life. Once I made the changes, I felt lighter. More positive. My anxiety lessened almost immediately."

Suddenly, the plane shifted and jerked.

"Attention passengers," a voice from the intercom announced. "We're going through some turbulence. Please stay seated and make sure your seatbelts are fastened."

Robert looked over to Treb as he buckled up his seatbelt. "That wasn't easy either—on my stomach that is."

"You need to meditate more," Treb said, as he buckled his seatbelt.

"So what's your life like now? How many positive and negative people do you have?" Robert asked.

"I haven't done the exercise in about a year. My guess is maybe eight out of ten people in my life are positive. The negative ones are there simply because of the relationship. But I can balance the energy now. Here's the thing—after you have been doing this for a while, you begin to build up almost like a force field to negative energy. Once you have enough positive energy, you can handle the small bits of negative energy that come your way."

"So you can stop worrying about negative energy?"

The plane jerked again in the turbulence.

"Even energy like that?" Robert said, referring to the shifting of the plane.

"Well, I add to my positivity bank every day," Treb said. "I listen to positive podcasts. I surround myself with positive people. I read positive books, stories, magazines. I read positive quotes. I'm always depositing. When some negative energy comes my way, my positive bank is so built up that one negative thing won't take me off track.

"One of the really positive people I have interviewed is Rick Hansen. He's Canadian and uses a wheelchair. He did this Man in Motion tour, where he travelled across Canada in his wheelchair, raising money and awareness to create a world without barriers for disabled people. Someone once suggested to me that Rick Hansen was just naturally inspired; he didn't have to work at it. So I thought I'd ask him about it. Rick was an Olympic hopeful before an accident in his teens left him paralyzed. When I asked him if he'd always been positive, he surprised me. He described himself as in a very dark place after the accident happened. He told me he had to work on his positivity every day. In fact, he and Terry Fox—another inspirational Canadian—used to call each other every day to inspire one another."

"Impressive," Robert said.

"Yes," Treb said. "It's like staying physically fit. It's a constant process."

Action for Lesson 6:
Be careful who you surround yourself with.

1. List the people you spend time with. Consider if they bring more positive or negative energy into your life.

Chapter 11:

HAPPY MONEY

"**D**o you have happy money?" Treb asked.

"Do I have what?"

"Happy money."

"I'm not sure. What is happy money?"

"I'm glad you asked. Another person I've met is Ken Honda. He's a bestselling author in Japan. After retiring at a young age, he wrote like fifty books on wealth and personal development. One time, he was at a networking event. He was talking to lady he'd just met, and she asked if she could see inside his wallet. Ken was curious, so he handed it over. She started leafing through his bills, looking them over. Then, she switched the order of the bills, handed him back his wallet, and said, 'Good, you have happy money.' He asked what happy money was. She explained it was money that's not tied to guilt or resentment. It's earned by integrity-based means by serving one's purpose."

The plane jolted yet again in the turbulence.

"That's hard on the stomach," Robert said.

Treb paused until the plane settled again.

"Ken walked away from the conversation wanting to learn more about happy money and to help others have wallets filled with it."

"That's intriguing," Robert said.

"I agree. Money is energy. Well, everything is energy. So money can carry happy or unhappy energy depending how it was acquired and how its owner feels about it," Treb said. "So do you have happy money, Robert?"

Robert took a long pause. "I'm not sure I do. What can I do to get it?"

"Well, I'd recommend checking out Ken Honda's work. But I'll tell you one thing I changed after learning about this thing he calls happy money."

"Great!"

"Well, I believe having a good relationship with money means being grateful for it. Like I said earlier, if you were born in North America and have a job at a fast-food restaurant, you're earning more than half of the rest of the world. Being grateful for what we have includes the money we have. Maybe we should communicate with it."

"You talk to your money?" Robert asked.

"Yes. Ken told me to start saying *arigato* to my money. So I do, whenever I spend or get it."

"Wait, isn't that from the 'Mr. Roboto' song?" Robert asked.

"Isn't what from the 'Mr. Roboto' song?"

"That word," Robert explained.

"Maybe. The song sounds familiar."

"Well, what does it have to do with money? Why would you look at money and say the 'Mr. Roboto' word?"

"Well, I'm not sure if it's in the song. But it means *thank you*. The idea is to look at physical or digital money and express gratitude. Whether you say *thank you* or *arigato* is up to you."

All of a sudden, the captain came over the loudspeaker. "Attention passengers—we may have to make an unscheduled landing. We have a gas leak. Given the turbulence, we need to land immediately. In the meantime, I would consider whether you have fully lived your life."

Everyone in the plane went quiet with shock.

Chapter 12:
THE LAST FLIGHT?

After what seemed like forever, the captain came back on the loudspeaker. "Did I get your attention? Make you think about how you've been living your life?" he asked. "We are still in the middle of a rough area, but we are not making an unscheduled landing and we don't have a gas leak. Aren't you relieved?"

Chatter started to build throughout the cabin. "Well, that pilot is done," said a lady in one of the seats ahead of Robert and Treb.

"What a jerk!" Robert said. "I can't believe he just did that." Robert shook his head and looked back to Treb. "Let's get back to our chat. Where were we? Lesson 7?"

"Lesson 7," confirmed Treb. "Well, I already mentioned gratitude and a gratitude journal. Lesson 7 is about finding ways to practise your gratitude.

"For example, Gina likes the journal idea. She'll get up even before I do, head out onto the back deck with her coffee, sit down on one of our deck chairs, and list five things she's grateful for."

"Five things? Does she ever run out?"

"Well, yes and no. She tries to include new things. But I know she sometimes lists things she might have been grateful for a month before."

"I'm not much of a journal writer, Treb," Robert said. "What else have you got?"

"A gratitude jar. This is what I do. Every day, I write three things I'm grateful for on a slip of paper. I put the paper in the jar. At the end of the year, I pull out the slips and read them to remind myself how lucky I am. I find the more I express gratitude, the more things I ultimately receive that I can be grateful for."

"A gratitude jar, huh? Sounds simple enough."

"Gina also takes pictures of one thing she is grateful for each day. Then, after she has taken enough pictures, she'll makes a collage. With this method, you can look at the collage and see what you are grateful for. I look at her collages sometimes, and they remind me of things I'm grateful for, too."

"Anything else?"

"Meditation," Treb said.

"Meditation again? It's mixed with gratitude now?"

"Well, sort of. It's a different kind of meditation. It's a gratitude meditation. I write down the things I'm grateful for, and then I sit to meditate. I think about the things I've written down. So it's like a normal meditation, but rather than just being present, I focus on being grateful."

"Is this a new thing?"

"Not at all. There's this meditation guy, Jack Kornfield. He talks about how people in different spiritual traditions start the day by expressing chants or prayers of gratitude."

"Interesting," Robert replied.

Before Robert could continue chatting, a man walking up the aisle from the front cabin bathroom stopped in front of him. "Hey, aren't you that guy from that movie, with the kid who ..." the man started to say. Then, he took a longer look at Robert's face. "Oh, sorry. Never mind. My mistake. I thought you were somebody famous."

"I'm important enough to be sitting in a better class than you!" Robert said. He wasn't used to someone talking to him that way. The other passenger turned red with embarrassment and made his way back to his seat.

Treb looked at Robert and shook his head.

"What?" Robert asked. "That guy insulted me."

"I guess it's time for Lesson 8," Treb said with a sigh.

Actions for Lesson 7:
Practice an attitude of gratitude.

1. Say arigato or thank you for the money in your life.
2. Write in a gratitude journal, use a gratitude jar, or create a gratitude collage.

Chapter 13:
THE PLATINUM RULE

"**L**et's talk more about *Think and Grow Rich*," Treb said.

"Sure," Robert replied. He was still eager to know more about the *rich* part.

"Years ago, I was asked to write chapters in another book series about *Think and Grow Rich*. The books had authors giving their interpretation of a chapter from the original. One of the chapters I focused on was one of Hill's most underappreciated teachings."

"What was that?" Robert asked.

"I believe he said something like, 'The man who does more than he is paid for will soon be paid for more than he does.' I started living like this, trying to do more for others than I expected to receive back."

"How does that relate to how I treated that rude passenger?" Robert asked.

"Well, if you do more for others than they expect, you also have to forgive people—especially for small things. Remember I said earlier that you shouldn't worry about something that won't matter in ten years?"

"Yes."

"I'm pretty sure you won't remember that passenger confusing you for someone else in ten hours, let alone ten years. To really over-deliver for people, you need to treat them better than they treat you."

"So what's Lesson 8?" Robert asked. "Be the bigger person?"

"It's so much larger than that."

"Can you give me a hint?"

"It's more about figuring out how to love others without condition, how to understand that everyone is doing the best with what they know. How about I give you a way to practise the lesson?"

"Finally," Robert said with a smile, "something practical again."

"Have you ever heard of the Golden Rule?"

"Sure," Robert replied. "Do unto others as you would have them do unto you."

"Lesson 8 is what I call the Platinum Rule. Using the Golden Rule, you treat people how *you* want to be treated. Using the Platinum Rule, you treat people how *they* want to be treated. You try to treat people how they want to be treated, based on their preferences, interests, and the like."

"But isn't that more work?"

"I guess it depends what you consider work. I feel better when I help people. If I can do it in the way that most pleases them, I get just as much reward as they do. So to me, it isn't work."

"But it helps your pocketbook, too, I bet," Robert said.

"I think you'll find it's so much bigger than the pocketbook."

"But it also helps the pocketbook, doesn't it?" Robert persisted.

"Sometimes it's not about the reward. Have you ever heard the story about the wolf and the crane?"

"I don't think so."

"I think it's a fable by Aesop, who was a slave and storyteller in ancient Greece. Basically, the story is about a wolf with a bone stuck in its throat. The wolf convinces a crane to help dislodge the bone. The crane helps but asks for its reward. The wolf says something like, 'You have put your head inside a wolf's mouth and taken it out again in safety; that should be enough reward.'"

Robert thought for a minute. "What the heck does that mean?"

"Meditate on it over the next couple of days. I suspect you'll figure it out."

"I do give to others," Robert said. "I donate to charity."

"That's great. Tithing is a powerful way to give thanks for your abundance and give to others who are in need."

"What's tithing?" Robert asked.

"It describes giving a percentage, typically a tenth, of what you have to support someone else."

"Oh," Robert said, nodding his head.

"And it's a good thing," Treb said. "But you know what's just as important as being a good giver?"

Robert shrugged.

"Being a good receiver. Many people really struggle with receiving. But being a good receiver is also a way to serve others."

Robert looked puzzled. "Wait a minute. How can I serve a person while taking from them?"

"Seems counterintuitive, right?"

"It sure does."

"Let me give you an example. One time, I had just delivered a keynote presentation at a large venue. After my talk, I was backstage in the green room with the other speakers and their friends. I was engaging in some small talk with a couple of the other speakers, when a musician approached me. I won't get into name-dropping …"

"This is the first time you're not saying a name, so now I want to know!" Robert said with a laugh.

"Well, let's just say I was a huge fan. I was starstruck. The musician actually apologized for interrupting, and to my surprise, he wanted to chat. He went on to say how much he loved my talk and how one of the lessons would change his life. I was such a big fan, so I did what many of us do. I started diminishing the compliments by saying things like, 'Oh, you're far too kind, it wasn't my best talk,' and the like. Here he was trying to give me a compliment, and I essentially discounted it because I felt embarrassed by it.

"I didn't really think about it until later that day. When I was about to leave the green room, I went over to compliment one of the other speakers. That speaker was also embarrassed and tried to deflect my compliment. I realized that the speaker had robbed me of the feeling of giving by brushing off my compliment, but I had done the same to the musician. I had robbed the musician of the experience of giving. It made me realize how tied together giving and receiving are."

"Wow," Robert exclaimed. "I just realized I suck at receiving. I do the same thing. I like it when someone accepts a gift from me. If I don't do the same, I'm actually taking away from the thoughtful person. So how would you summarize Lesson 8?" Robert asked.

"Well, it's about loving unconditionally. But I think a great start is to practise the Platinum Rule and be a great giver and receiver."

"So powerful," Robert said, as he looked down at his watch. "We've been talking for hours! I can't believe there's barely an hour left on the flight. I've really enjoyed our conversation. I usually prefer to sleep or work rather than chat."

"You? I never would have guessed," Treb said. "I've enjoyed chatting as well. Mind you, I did a lot of the talking."

Actions for Lesson 8:
Practice the Platinum Rule.

1. Treat people as they would like to be treated.
2. Be a good giver AND receiver.

Chapter 14:

ONE PERCENT BETTER

T hough Robert was enjoying his chat with Treb, he was also a bit sore from sitting so long. He stretched out his legs in front of him and then put his hands on the back of his neck to massage out some of the kinks.

Then he turned back to Treb. "Okay," he said. "Let's get to Lesson 9."

Treb started with another question. "Have you ever thought how hockey players like Sidney Crosby and Wayne Gretzky and basketball players like Michael Jordan have coaches that can't do what those players have done?"

"Sure," Robert replied.

"Me too. One time on a flight, I was seated next to an elite skating coach. He had worked with the likes of Crosby and Gretzky. Not on hockey, but on skating. So I asked what someone could possibly teach Gretzky about something he did ninety-nine percent perfectly?"

"What did he say?"

"He said people like Gretzky work with coaches on seemingly small things because they want to figure out tiny changes to help them with that last one percent. The real chance for improvement is in that last one percent. People like Gretzky, who are at top of their fields, aren't content to leave that one percent on the table."

"I never thought about that before."

"Most people haven't. But when you realize the areas where you can improve, you can make a conscious effort to become better in that area. That's where real change can happen."

"Do you have any suggestions for figuring out a person's improvement areas?"

"A great place to start is to ask people for feedback. What do you do well? What could you improve? That kind of thing. Hearing about your strengths will help you realize how you create value for others. Hearing things you could improve will help you put together a list of the areas where you could be doing the work. Your one percent. But whether it's asking people to share their thoughts on social media or a one-on-one conversation, you have to make yourself vulnerable enough to ask."

"And what about doing the work?"

"For someone like you, such a goal-driven person, you likely just need to commit to working on those areas. For most people, it comes back to creating good habits. Here's what I did. After I spoke to the skating coach, I knew I needed to figure out what I needed to improve. I'm part of this mastermind group, and we were all together in Costa Rica. I just asked if I could have the floor for a minute. And I asked my fellow masterminders if they would be open to give me input on my weaknesses and strengths if I sent out a survey. They agreed. The next week, I emailed them all the survey."

"A survey? Did they fill it out?"

"Most did. But this is a group I interact with regularly."

"Did their answers surprise you?"

"Some did. Some didn't. But as soon as I saw the responses, I knew they were spot-on. It was kind of like the weaknesses were right in front of my face, but I needed someone else to point them out! Then I started habits to improve."

"Can you give me an example?" Robert asked.

"Sure. It came up that I wasn't so great at delegating."

"Oh, I hate delegating," Robert said. "It's *so* much more work than just doing it yourself. The person you give the job to always has questions. And they won't do it as well."

"I struggled with the feedback at first, but I realized it was true. I wasn't good at delegating. If you're not a good receiver, you rob the other person of giving. And if you're not good at delegating, you rob the other person of opportunities. They don't get a feeling of empowerment or a feeling that I trust them. They don't get the chance to build their skills."

"I never thought of it like that before," Robert said.

"I didn't change overnight. I started by delegating just one thing a day to someone else. I picked small things at first. And I even rewarded myself for delegating."

"Why?" Robert asked.

"Human beings like rewards. They motivate us. I was simply trying to encourage more good behavior. So every day, I delegated one thing and then rewarded myself until it became a habit. Then I found myself delegating more work, more often. A year later, I felt like delegating was my superpower."

"Anything else I should know about working on my one percent?"

"Hire a good coach. Top athletes and influencers have coaches. You should have one too. It's better if you know your one percent focus area first, but you can let the coach have some input.

"You can also do a running inventory of your days," Treb added.

"An inventory every day?"

"It's easier than it sounds. Basically, at the start of each day or the night before, you plan your activities. Then at the end of the day, you do an inventory of how your day went. You know, things you did well, things you would change."

"Do I have to do all of this to be successful?"

"Well, it sounds like you're already successful. But this stuff will help you grow and evolve. T. Harv Eker wrote *Secrets of the Millionaire Mind*. He says if you show him a person's bank balance and habits, he can tell you almost to the dollar how much that person will have in the bank in ten years. Unless the person changes their habits, that is. He says people have a money blueprint. Unless they change that, they will get the same results in ten years that they have today. Life is the same way. If you don't change your blueprint, your life will likely look the same in ten years as it does today."

Robert nodded. He knew Treb was right. He looked at his watch again. "My mind is so full. I feel lucky to have you sitting next to me on this flight. I don't use the word *grateful* often. Actually, I never do. But I'm grateful for this conversation. Maybe it was even *synchronicity* that we were seated together."

"I'm sure it was," Treb said.

"We only have about fifty minutes left, and I haven't heard Lesson 10. I would also love to exchange contact info, if that's cool? I know you and Gina still travel; I travel a lot, too. I'd love to see if we could meet up for dinner sometime."

"Gina would love that," Treb said.

Actions for Lesson 9:
Focus on your one percent.

1. Do an inventory of your strengths & weaknesses.
2. Hire the right coach.
3. Do a beginning-of-day and end-of-day inventory.
4. Work to reset your blueprint.

Chapter 15:

GET A DOG

"**B**y the way, you should get a dog," Treb said. "You said you're too busy for one, but you should get a dog."

"Is that Lesson 10?" Robert asked. "Get a dog?"

"No, I'll get to that in a minute," Treb said with a laugh.

"I live in a high-rise. I can't get a dog," Robert said.

"Well, just keep it in mind. Pets add happiness to your life. You might also want to read about other things that can add to your life. A guy named Dan Buettner actually identified five what he called 'blue zones,' places in the world where people live longer. He found things they had in common—like purpose, belonging, connections, movement, how they eat, and other things. He wanted to share the information with the rest of the world."

"You're not going to go through all five blue zones, are you? My head is mush," Robert admitted.

"Maybe that's for a different flight," Treb agreed. "But you should check out his books. You should also check out a guy named Rob Dubin and his talk on happiness. He talks about how when we're growing we're happier, and how we need to continue to find ways to grow personally if we want to be happier. It's such a powerful talk. Oh, and you should get a dog. Gina and I have Lego."

"Lego? I like that name."

"We do too."

"So what about Lesson 10?"

"Don't worry, my young friend. Just let me go to the bathroom first. We'll get you that lesson."

"I'll hold you to that," Robert said, pointing at Treb. "By the way, do you have kids?" he added.

Treb smiled but did not answer. He just got up from his seat and made his way to the back of the plane.

"You know you can go in the front? You're in first class."

Treb continued toward the bathroom in the rear of the plane.

"Kind of an eccentric old fella," Robert said, as he shifted in his seat to get comfortable. Then, he leaned back and closed his eyes, trying to soak in the knowledge he'd heard. *Is this meditation?* he thought. Within a few minutes, he had fallen asleep.

Robert didn't wake until the plane jolted to its landing. He sat straight up in his seat, then looked out the window to see the runway, and to the left to see an empty seat beside him. He had no intention of falling asleep! And where was Treb?

Robert pushed the button above his seat to call the flight attendant. Within seconds, she was at his seat. "I'm sorry, Mr. Stapleton, but service has ended, and I'm really not supposed to be walking around the plane during landing. How can I help you?"

"I'm just worried about my seatmate," he said, pointing to the empty seat next to him. "He hasn't come back from the bathroom. Is he okay?"

"Your seatmate? There hasn't been anyone sitting in this seat for the entire flight, Mr. Stapleton. If I recall, you requested that no one be seated next to you. Are you feeling okay, Mr. Stapleton?"

Robert didn't respond to the flight attendant before she left for the front to begin the deplaning process. Passengers started standing up and pulling down their luggage from the overhead bins, but Robert sat in a blur. How could Treb *not* have been sitting next to him? His head was full of the life lessons Treb had taught him. Robert couldn't have dreamed all of that. Could he?

What other explanation could there be? Robert thought.

As he made his way down the aisle toward the front of the plane, Robert spoke to the lady walking in front of him. "Excuse me, did you happen to see me talking to someone during the flight?" Robert asked.

"No, I'm sorry, she said, turning back toward him while continuing to walk along the passenger boarding bridge. "I assumed you were asleep. The flight was so quiet!"

"Thank you," he replied. He was completely dumbfounded. It had all seemed so real.

Robert walked into the airport for his next flight. As he proceeded through the terminal, he started to become more aware of his surroundings. He had another flight to catch and he usually liked to be early, so he began rushing toward security. Once he arrived, he was greeted by an overwhelming number of indifferent or grumpy faces. *Air travel tests people with even the best of dispositions*, he thought.

"Passport and boarding pass, please," said the lady in the uniform at the front of security.

Robert handed over his passport and boarding pass. The woman in uniform glanced at them, then handed both back and yelled, "Next!" He walked to the conveyer belt and placed his laptop, carry-on, keys, and other items into the security bins. Then he swung around toward the metal detector for the security check.

As he turned, he crashed right into a woman with a mass of curly blonde hair and wearing a bright red dress. He jolted back to apologize.

"Oh wow, I'm so sorry," Robert said. "I wasn't looking where I was walking and …" he trailed off. *She was beautiful.* "I'm just so sorry …" he repeated, leaving the sentence open as if to leave room for her name.

"Gina," she said, extending her hand to shake his. "Don't worry. I wasn't paying that much attention either."

Gina? Wasn't that Treb's wife's name?

Robert looked down and saw an envelope on the ground. Thinking that Gina must have dropped it, he leaned over to pick it up. As he grabbed the envelope, a piece of paper fell out with the name Diane on it.

Wait a minute. Didn't Treb say he met his Gina in an airport? Wasn't his mother's name Diane? How did I not even remember my mother's middle name is Diane?

Robert handed the envelope to Gina.

And didn't Treb say he once worked in the same job as I do now? And he had the same watch? And the Om tattoo? It had more detail and looked older, but couldn't it have been added to? He sounds like an older me!

Was I dreaming of my future self?

Gina finally tapped Robert on the shoulder and pulled him from all of his questions. "Any chance you're up for getting a bite to eat before the next flight?"

Robert paused to answer. And before he could reply, Gina pointed at the floor behind him. "You dropped a paper too."

He looked back, prepared to say he hadn't been carrying a paper. But sure enough, there was a folded piece of paper lying on the ground behind him. Curious, he turned around, leaned over, grabbed the paper, and opened it up.

Ten Lessons for a Rich Life

Lesson 1: *Embrace the power of synchronicity. The more you notice and act on synchronicities, the more they occur.*

Lesson 2: *Enjoy the journey and the destination.*

Lesson 3: *Make 'no' a new mantra.*

Lesson 4: *Live each day like it's your last (but plan like it's not).*

Lesson 5: *Mindset is everything.*

Lesson 6: *Be careful who you surround yourself with.*

Lesson 7: *Practise an attitude of gratitude.*

Lesson 8: *Practise the Platinum Rule.*

Lesson 9: *Focus on your one percent.*

Lesson 10: *Stay open to the wonders of life (and say yes to the bite to eat)!*

* Learn more about living like people in the blue zones.

And again, I say to you, my younger friend—live fully, die empty! Most importantly, write a book sharing these lessons. Share the book with everyone and ask them to share it with everyone they know. You never know when your book could impact, or transform, a life.

After scanning the lessons, Robert folded the piece of paper back up and tucked it safely into his suit jacket pocket.

"I'd love to," he said, finally replying to Gina's invitation to have a bite to eat.

"Great," Gina said. "I don't know the airport. This is my first flight."

READING LIST

John Assaraf, https://www.myneurogym.com/

Les Brown, https://lesbrown.com/

Dan Buettner, *The Blue Zones*, https://www.bluezones.com/

Warren Buffet, https://www.berkshirehathaway.com/

Rhonda Byrne, *The Secret*, https://www.thesecret.tv/products/the-secret-book/

Jack Canfield, https://jackcanfield.com/

Paulo Coelho, *The Alchemist*, HarperCollins

Davidji, https://davidji.com/

Rob Dubin, https://www.robdubin.com/

Terry Fox, https://terryfox.org/terrys-story/

Héctor García, *Ikigai: The Japanese Secret to a Long and Happy Life*, https://hectorgarcia.org/

Stedman Graham, https://stedmangraham.com/

Buddy Guy, https://www.buddyguy.net/

Mark Victor Hansen, https://markvictorhansen.com/

Rick Hansen, https://www.rickhansen.com/

Darren Hardy, *The Compound Effect*, https://darrenhardy.com/

Napoleon Hill, *Think and Grow Rich*, https://www.naphill.org/

Ken Honda, https://kenhonda.com/

Jack Kornfield, https://jackkornfield.com/

Natalie and Glen Ledwell, Mind Movies, https://www.mindmovies.com/

Shannon Lee, *Be Water My Friend: The Teachings of Bruce Lee, Flatiron Books*

Lisa Nichols, https://motivatingthemasses.com/

Cappi Pidwell, https://www.cappipidwell.com/home_thecappipid
    wellmethod

Bob Proctor, https://www.proctorgallagherinstitute.com/

James Redfield, *The Celestine Prophecy*, https://www.celestinevision.com/

Tony Robbins, https://www.tonyrobbins.com/

Don Miguel Ruiz, *The Four Agreements,* https://www.miguelruiz.com/

Don Miguel Ruiz Jr., https://www.miguelruiz.com/

Robin Sharma, *The Monk Who Sold His Ferrari*,
    https://www.robinsharma.com/

Marci Shimoff, https://happyfornoreason.com/

Eckhart Tolle, *The Power of Now*, https://eckharttolle.com/

Neale Donald Walsch, http://www.nealedonaldwalsch.com/

Wallace Wattles, *The Science of Getting Rich*

Zig Ziglar, https://www.ziglar.com/

ABOUT THE AUTHOR

Corey Poirier is a TEDx speaker, host of the top-rated *Let's Do Influencing* radio show, and founder of the growing bLU Talks brand. *Success* magazine recently named him as one of fifteen emerging entrepreneurs.

Corey is a Barnes and Noble, Amazon, Apple Books, and Kobo bestselling author; award-winning author; and co-author of *The Wall Street Journal/*USA Today bestseller *Quitless*.

He has interviewed more than 6,500 of the world's top leaders, including Ken Honda, Lisa Nichols, Dr. Shefali, Deepak Chopra, Tommy Chong, Neale Donald Walsch, Marie Diamond, and Kristina Mänd-Lakhiani, is a columnist with *Entrepreneur* and *Forbes* magazines, and he has also spoken onsite at events at Harvard, Columbia, MIT, UCLA, Stanford, and Cambridge, and more recently to Microsoft team leaders and at Kyle Wilson's Inner Circle retreat.

Also appearing on the popular Evan Carmichael YouTube channel, Corey has been named a New Media Summit Icon of Influence, a top five influencer in entrepreneurship by Thinkers 360, and a 2021 Brainz CREA Global Honoree.

Showing his versatility, he is also a rock recording of the year nominee who has performed stand-up comedy more than 700 times, including an appearance at the famed Second City.

A free ebook edition is available with the purchase of this book.

To claim your free ebook edition:

1. Visit MorganJamesBOGO.com
2. Sign your name CLEARLY in the space
3. Complete the form and submit a photo of the entire copyright page
4. You or your friend can download the ebook to your preferred device

A **FREE** ebook edition is available for you or a friend with the purchase of this print book.

_____

CLEARLY SIGN YOUR NAME ABOVE

Instructions to claim your free ebook edition:
1. Visit MorganJamesBOGO.com
2. Sign your name CLEARLY in the space above
3. Complete the form and submit a photo of this entire page
4. You or your friend can download the ebook to your preferred device

Print & Digital Together Forever.

Snap a photo

Free ebook

Read anywhere

9 781636 984407